D0772699

istening to my Body:
 guide to helping kids understand the connection
etween sensations (what the heck are those?) and
eelings so that they can get better at figuring out
vhat they need.

By Gabi Garcia

Illustrated by Ying Hui Tan

For Liliana

skinned knee
publishing

902 Gardner Road No. 4
Austin, TX 78721

Copyright 2016, 2017 Gabi Garcia
Illustrations by Ying Hui Tan

Second Edition: July 2017
First Edition: August 2016
Paperback ISBN: 978-0-9989580-0-2
Hardcover ISBN: 978-0-9989580-1-9
eBook ISBN 978-0-9989580-2-6

Publisher's Cataloging-In-Publication Data

Names: Garcia, Gabi. | Tan, YingHui, illustrator.
Title: Listening to my body : a guide to helping kids understand the connection between their sensations (what the heck are those?) and feelings so that they can get better at figuring out what they need / by Gabi Garcia ; illustrated by Ying Hui Tan.
Description: Second edition. | Austin, TX : Take Heart Press, 2017. | Interest age level: 004-008. | Summary: "Listening to My Body is an engaging and interactive picture book that introduces children to the practice of paying attention to their bodies. Through a combination of story, and simple experiential activities, it guides them through the process of noticing and naming their feelings and the physical sensations that accompany them so that they can build on their capacity to engage mindfully, self-regulate and develop a deeper sense of well-being."--Provided by publisher.
Identifiers: ISBN 978-0-9989580-0-2 (paperback) | ISBN 978-0-9989580-1-9 (hardcover) | ISBN 978-0-9989580-2-6 (ebook)
Subjects: LCSH: Mind and body--Juvenile literature. | Emotions--Juvenile literature. | Mindfulness (Psychology)--Juvenile literature. | Self-care, Health--Juvenile literature. | CYAC: Mind and body. | Emotions. | Mindfulness (Psychology) | Self-care, Health.
Classification: LCC BF149.5 .G37 2017 (print) | LCC BF149.5 (ebook) | DDC 150--dc23

A note to parents and teachers

I firmly believe that teaching children to tune into and trust their bodies is a lifelong gift. To that end, I have created *Listening to My Body*, a book intended to help children develop an awareness of what their bodies are telling them. This book will help them understand the connection between sensations and feelings and teach them to practice identifying and naming what they are experiencing, so they can get better at figuring out what they need.

The "Let's Practice" activities at the bottom of some pages are experiential and designed to help kids practice what they are learning. I invite and encourage you to read the book and do the activities ahead of time for yourself so that you are familiar with them. Give children plenty of time as you guide them through these activities. Alternately, if a child chooses not to practice an activity, they can return to it at a later time.

A list of sensation and feeling words is provided at the end of this book to give children the language to describe what they are experiencing. Some activities from the book are also listed there so that children can practice them and decide which feel good to them, or help them feel calm, peaceful or relaxed.

There are many ways you can continue to support your child to "listen" to their body. You can:

Build a vocabulary of sensation words. Start with the one found in the book and build from there.

Help them further connect their sensations and feelings. When they identify a feeling, you can ask questions like, "How does your body tell you that you are happy, excited, angry, etc.?" or "Where in your body do you notice the calm, sad, nervous, etc. feeling?"

Model the process of "listening" to your body and showing care and kindness for yourself.

Visit www.gabigarciabooks.com for downloadable resources to accompany this book.

Warmly,
Gabi

My body is my friend!

It tells me lots of things.

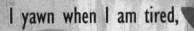
I yawn when I am tired,

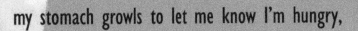
my stomach growls to let me know I'm hungry,

and sometimes I get goosebumps when I'm cold.

This happens on its own, without me doing anything. I may not even notice that it's happening, but I can start paying attention to my body and so can you.

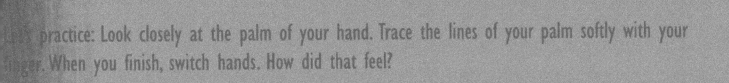
Let's practice: Look closely at the palm of your hand. Trace the lines of your palm softly with your finger. When you finish, switch hands. How did that feel?

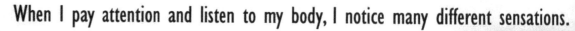
When I pay attention and listen to my body, I notice many different sensations.

Sensations are the physical feelings we all have inside and outside our bodies.

Cold, sweaty, strong, and **breathless** are examples of sensations.
Have you felt these sensations before?

Let's practice. Rub your hands together quickly for thirty seconds. What do you notice? Heat?
Tingles? Sweat? Anything else? Those are sensations.

The sensations in my body are always changing. There are times when my body is so wiggly and squirmy that it's like I have ants in my pants.

At other times, my body is calm and still.

Sometimes the beat of my heart is like a gentle tap.

Sometimes it feels like a pounding drum!

Let's practice. Place your hand over your heart and see if you feel its beat (it's okay if you can't). Now, jump up and down quickly 15 times. Place your hand on your heart again. What happened to your heartbeat? Did it change or stay the same? Do you notice anything else? Like a change in your temperature or your breathing?

I can also listen to my body for clues about how I'm feeling about the things happening around me. Feelings are not good or bad. They're something we all experience.

Curious, proud, grumpy, and **scared** are a few feelings we all have.
What other feelings can you name?

What I've learned from listening to my body is that sensations and feelings go together. I noticed thi[s] when I got to ride a rollercoaster for the first time. I was super excited that I was finally tall enough to ride it, but I also felt nervous as I climbed on board. My belly felt squishy and fluttery.

My mom calls that having butterflies in your stomach, but I thought it felt more like a kitty chasing ping pong balls in there.

What sensations do you notice when you're excited or nervous?

When I got off the rollercoaster, I was buzzing and tingly all over. My eyes were like saucers and I had a smile plastered on my face.

I felt awesome!

Let's practice. Place your hand on your belly and take ten deep breaths. Notice your belly as it moves in and out with each breath. How does your belly feel? Soft? Relaxed? Tight? Something else?

Sometimes when I'm sad, I get a lump in my throat that makes it hard to talk or breathe. Soon, warm tears roll down my face, and I may start to cry harder. Crying makes me feel better. So do hugs.

We all feel sad at times. **What do you need when you're sad?**

t's practice. Wrap your arms around yourself and give yourself a gentle hug. Move your hands up
d down your arms. Squeeze a little tighter and find what feels best for you. Do you like a tight
g or a gentle squeeze?

My mom once explained to me that sensations and feelings are like the waves in the ocean. Some come crashing in, while others roll in gently, and they always come and go. We can't stop the waves from coming, but we can pay attention to them so they don't knock us over.

Sometimes my skin gets burning hot and my jaw and fists feel hard as rocks. That happened to my body the last time I got really angry at my sister. She'd just destroyed the puzzle I was working on all afternoon.

I stomped my feet and slammed the door, but I really wanted to **kick it!**

But then I remembered to take deep breaths and blow out through my lips like a horse and it didn't take long for my jaw and hands to relax, and for my skin to cool down.

The angry feeling and sensations faded away. Blowing "horse lips" even made me feel a little silly and it tickled.

I decided to put the puzzle on a table that my sister couldn't reach.

Let's practice. Close your mouth so that your lips touch gently. Inhale through your nose and blow a strong puff of air through your mouth so that your lips flap like a horse's. Try that a couple of times. What do you notice? How do your lips and jaw feel?

Sometimes I get overwhelmed and need help from a grown-up. On the first day of school, I woke up super early because I couldn't stop thinking about what my new class would be like. My stomach felt like it was tied in knots so I didn't eat breakfast.

In class, it was hard for me to focus on what my new teacher, Ms. Morgan was saying, and my body was shaky. When it was time to line up, I accidentally bumped my desk and knocked my stuff all over the floor. Everything was going wrong!

. Morgan helped me pick up my things and I took deep breaths like she reminded me to. I told her out my morning and she explained that our brains have a hard time thinking when our bodies are ed and hungry. Ms. Morgan thought I would feel better if I had a snack and rested in a quiet place ile the class was at recess.

e was right! When I came back to the classroom, I was calm and able to focus so the rest of my y went much better.

okay to get help when we need it. Who is an adult that helps you?

At other times when I'm upset, I can figure out what I need on my own by listening to my body. I can pay attention to my breathing, my heartbeat, the temperature of my skin, or to any other sensation.

Am I hungry or thirsty? Tired or full of energy? Is my belly tense and tight or soft and relaxed? These are just some questions I can ask myself.

I can also try to name my feelings. Do I feel peaceful or playful? Confused, or frustrated? Hurt, or cranky? There are many different ways I may be feeling and they are all okay.

Listening to my body and naming what I feel takes practice, but it helps me figure out what I need.

Do I need to have a snack, drink some water or get some rest? Do I need to take deep breaths or sing my favorite song? Do I need to sit in a quiet place alone or go outside and jump around?

I can color or draw, dance, cuddle with my dog or hang around someone I love. These are things I do that help me feel calm, happy or peaceful.

Everybody is different, so you get to decide what feels best for you.

The more I practice listening to my body, the better I get at responding with care and kindness for myself. I can get better at listening to my body, and so can **you!**

Let's practice: Listen to your body. Do you want to sit down or stand up? Do you need to be still or move around? Would you like to wiggle and jiggle, hop or dance? It's your body so you get to decide.

Move in a way that feels good to you!

Listen To Your Body

Below are sensations found in this book. Are there any others that you can add to this list? What sensations do you notice right now?

Ants in my pants	Breathless	Burning	Butterflies in your stomach	Calm
Cold	Cool	Fluttery	Focused	Full of energy	Goosebumps
Hot	Hungry	Lump in throat	Pounding	Relaxed	Shaky
Soft	Squirmy	Squishy	Still	Stomach growl	Strong	Sweaty	Tense
Thirsty	Tickles	Wiggly		

Below are feelings found in this book. Are there any others you can add to this list. What feelings do you notice right now?

Angry	Awesome	Calm	Cranky	Confused	Curious
Excited	Frustrated	Grumpy	Happy	Hurt	Lonely
Nervous	Overwhelmed	Peaceful	Playful	Proud	Sad
Safe	Scared	Silly	Upset		

PRACTICE

Below are activities found in this book that may feel good to your body or help you feel calm, peaceful or relaxed. Are there any more that you can add to this list? What do you need right now?

Have a snack	Go outside and jump around
Get a drink of water	Color or draw
Rest	Dance
Sing a song	Cuddle with a pet
Sit in a quiet place alone	Hang around someone you love

Place your hand on your belly and take 10 deep breaths. Feel your belly as it moves in and out. Notice how you feel.

Wrap your arms around yourself and give yourself a gentle hug. Move your hands up and down your arms. Squeeze a little tighter and find what feels best for you.

Close your mouth so that your lips touch gently. Inhale through your nose and blow a strong puff of air through your mouth so that your lips flap like a horse's. Try this a couple of times and notice how that feels.

Gabi Garcia is a mama, Licensed Professional Counselor and former teacher. She spent the last 20 years learning from the children she served in the public schools,.

She agrees that we teach what we most need to learn, and she always has better days when she listens to her body. Gabi lives with her family in Austin, Texas.

Visit gabigarciabooks.com for FREE downloadable resources to accompany this book.

  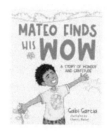  

OTHER BOOKS BY GABI GARCIA
ALL TITLES AVAILABLE IN SPANISH

Ying Hui Tan is a children's book illustrator. You can see more of her work at yinghuitan.com.

CPSIA information can be obtained
at www.ICGtesting.com
Printed in the USA
LVHW071030230822
726658LV00003B/43